Looking at . . . Vulcanodon

A Dinosaur from the JURASSIC Period

Weekly Reader BOOKS

Published by arrangement with Gareth Stevens, Inc.
Newfield Publications is a federally registered trademark
of Newfield Publications, Inc. Weekly Reader is a federally
registered trademark of Weekly Reader Corporation.

Library of Congress Cataloging-in-Publication Data available upon request from publisher.
Fax: (414) 225-0377 for the attention of the Publishing Records Department.

ISBN 0-8368-1350-2

This North American edition first published in 1995 by
Gareth Stevens Publishing
1555 North RiverCenter Drive, Suite 201
Milwaukee, Wisconsin 53212 USA

This U.S. edition © 1995 by Gareth Stevens, Inc. Created with original © 1995 by Quartz
Editorial Services, Premier House, 112 Station Road, Edgware HA8 7AQ U.K.

Consultant: Dr. David Norman, Director of the Sedgwick Museum of Geology,
University of Cambridge, England.

Additional artwork by Clare Herronneau.

Printed in the United States of America

Weekly Reader Books Presents

Looking at . . . Vulcanodon

A Dinosaur from the JURASSIC Period

by Heather Amery

Illustrated by Tony Gibbons

THE NEW
DINOSAUR
COLLECTION

Gareth Stevens Publishing
MILWAUKEE

Contents

Introducing
Vulcanodon

Large and lumbering, **Vulcanodon** (VUL-KAN-OH-DON) was a gentle giant that lived about 195 million years ago. It was probably too big for most meat-eating dinosaurs to attack easily. But if a greedy carnivore dared to grab at a baby **Vulcanodon** for a meal, it would have had to dodge the angry parents' stamping legs and lashing tails.

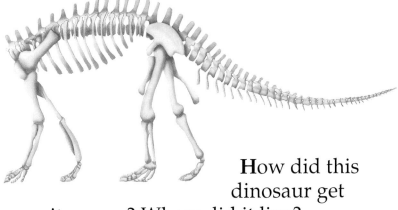

How did this dinosaur get its name? Where did it live? When were its fossilized bones first found? And how do we know what sort of meals it ate?

Normally peaceful, **Vulcanodon** nevertheless got angry if its offspring were threatened.

Scientists have discovered quite a bit about this prehistoric beast. But there are still some mysteries to be solved, as you will find out when you read on.

Bulky

What a thick body, heavy legs, long neck, and lengthy tail **Vulcanodon** had! From its nose to the tip of its tail, scientists think it must have measured about 21 feet (6.4 meters).

Stand on tiptoe and stretch up your arm; that was about the height of its shoulder. And its four pillarlike legs were even taller than you!

So it would have been about as long as a city bus. And, if it were not extinct, it would also be tall enough to look right over the top of the bus.

quadruped

Scientists have not yet been able to find out all they would like to know about this dinosaur, however. That's because the remains they have found are not complete. So the picture shown here is based on what many paleontologists believe it must have looked like.

Paleontologists think this Jurassic herbivore probably had a small head, with peglike teeth for pulling leaves from trees and other plants.

Because **Vulcanodon** had no flat teeth for chewing its food, it may also have swallowed small stones — not because these were delicious, but because they may have helped grind up the food in its stomach.

And if you could have slid along **Vulcanodon**'s long neck or tail, it might have been like speeding down a playground slide!

7

Incomplete skeleton

Digging up the skeleton of a new dinosaur is exciting work for scientists. They can learn a lot about prehistoric creatures from skeletons, even when some of the bones are missing.

By looking at the basic shape of the skeleton, scientists can figure out how big it was and how it walked. But when the fossilized bones of **Vulcanodon** were first dug up, the skeleton was not complete. Most of the bones of the body were there, but the head and neck had mysteriously disappeared, just as they are missing here.

8

What the paleontologists found, though, was that **Vulcanodon** had a very strong backbone. Powerful muscles, they guessed, probably supported a long neck.

They also found some spaces in the backbone. At one time, scientists thought large dinosaurs like **Vulcanodon** lived for some of the time in water and that these air-filled spaces in the backbone helped keep them afloat.

As you can see in the reconstruction shown here, **Vulcanodon** had a long tail that got thinner toward its end.

Its body was rounded and plump. The tail and neck together were probably more than twice the body length.

The long, straight leg bones showed that **Vulcanodon** walked on all four limbs. But its back legs were probably strong enough for **Vulcanodon** to stand almost upright on them to reach up for food or to fight with its front legs.

They later decided that such dinosaurs lived on land and that the spaces reduced the weight of their bones. With less weight to carry, they could move around more easily.

But until paleontologists manage to find **Vulcanodon**'s missing skull, of course, they can only make an intelligent guess about its head. The pictures in this book are based on their ideas.

9

Discovery in

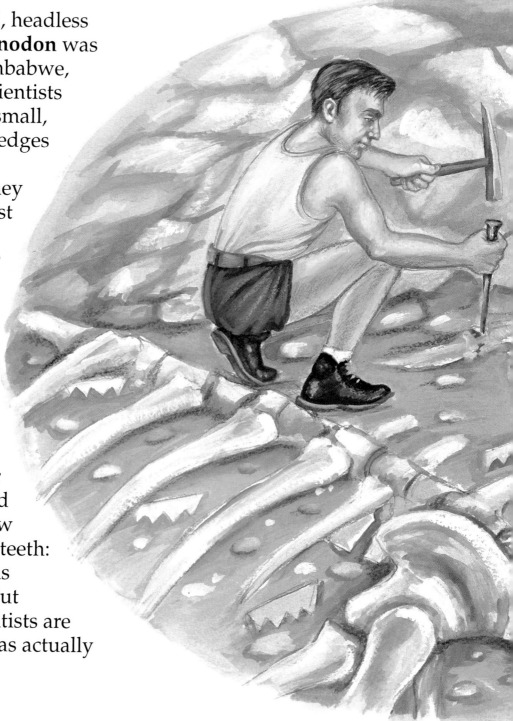

When a fossilized, headless skeleton of **Vulcanodon** was discovered in Zimbabwe, Africa, in 1972, scientists also found some small, sharp teeth, with edges like steak knives, nearby. At first, they thought these must have belonged to this new dinosaur and that it was a meat-eater.

Later, however, they changed their minds, deciding that the teeth must have been from another dinosaur. They had even called the new dinosaur after the teeth: **Vulcanodon** means "volcano tooth." But **Vulcanodon**, scientists are now convinced, was actually a herbivore.

Zimbabwe

The main problem with the **Vulcanodon** skeleton, though, was that the head and neck were completely missing. No one knows what happened to them — we can only imagine.

Vulcanodon's missing parts may have been eaten or dragged away by a hungry, scavenging dinosaur after **Vulcanodon** died. Or perhaps the bones were disturbed in some other way. Until a complete skeleton is found, scientists can only guess what this dinosaur really looked like. But they have more than enough evidence to be along the right lines.

A missing link?

Everyone was very excited by the discovery of **Vulcanodon** in Zimbabwe. This was not just another dinosaur that lived in herds during Jurassic times, but possibly a much more intriguing creature.

Vulcanodon seemed to belong to the **Sauropod** family — a group of giant plant-eating dinosaurs that lived about 195 million years ago. But it could perhaps have belonged to an earlier family group called the **Prosauropods** that lived between 230 and 195 million years ago. So was it perhaps the missing link between the two groups?

The **Prosauropods** were smaller dinosaurs than **Sauropods**. **Vulcanodon** was the size of a **Sauropod**, but its hips were like a **Prosauropod**. So **Vulcanodon** was probably on its way to becoming one of the true **Sauropods** — the largest living creatures ever to have walked on Earth.

Bringing dinosaurs to life

If you have seen the film *Jurassic Park*, you'll know that the story is about a group of scientists who create a dinosaur park on a remote Pacific island. They do this by taking dinosaur DNA from the blood of an insect that was trapped in amber, or fossilized sap, 150 million years ago. DNA is a sort of code in the cells of all living things. It causes babies to grow up to be the same creatures as their parents.

In *Jurassic Park*, the insect caught in the amber had bitten a dinosaur. This meant there was dinosaur DNA in its blood cells. In the film, this was used to grow dinosaurs millions of years after they became extinct.

But is this idea just fantasy? Or could it happen? Some scientists think it might be possible in the future. In 1994, they claimed to have succeeded in extracting dinosaur DNA from fossilized **Tyrannosaurus rex** (TIE-<u>RAN</u>-OH-<u>SAW</u>-RUS <u>RECKS</u>) bones. The next step is to grow DNA in living cells — but how?

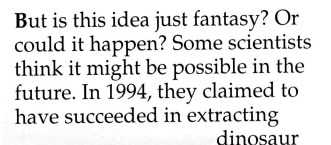

Dinosaurs' closest living relatives are birds, and the most logical to work with would be the largest — an ostrich — these scientists say.

They would first have to get DNA that came from a male and female of the same type of dinosaur. Then, they could try injecting the cells into ostrich eggs. When the eggs hatched, all the chicks would be ostriches — but some would have dinosaur "sex" cells.

After the chicks grew into adults and mated, the females would lay eggs. When these hatched, some would be ostriches, but some might be dinosaurs! For the moment, though, this is pure science fiction.

15

Looking after their young

It was early morning, and a herd of **Vulcanodon** was trampling a wide path through low trees and thick plant growth.

There were about twenty animals in the herd. In the lead was a large male that could reach to the top of the tallest trees. Behind him followed a group of younger males and females that protected several

They moved slowly in the warm sunshine, snatching the leaves off branches with their teeth as they ambled along. These were new feeding grounds, and the vegetation was abundant.

young babies in their midst. One baby, however, lagged behind. It was smaller and weaker than the other babies and could not keep up with the rest of the herd.

Its mother was the first to realize it was missing, and she slowed down the herd. It could not be left alone, for fear it might fall victim to a hungry predator craving a meal of young dinosaur flesh. Baby dinosaurs had perished in this way too often.

As the rest of the herd stopped to feed, the mother bent down to encourage her baby to move forward and catch up, tempting him with tidbits of fresh leaves and twigs.

The herd walked on, and all the mothers were now especially careful to keep the younger dinosaurs in the middle of their family group. There, they would be safe from attack.

Soon they came to a shallow pool. They stepped into the water to feed on the thick weeds growing along the banks, and to cool off from their journey. Even in the water, as good parents, they continued to protect the babies by surrounding them.

She could now hear what she recognized as the distant roar of a carnivore. It was vital that the young one did not lag behind.

If they were to survive the dangers of the Jurassic world, dinosaur babies needed close supervision.

Mating rituals

Vulcanodon probably lived in small family herds led by one big male. At the start of each mating season, the males fought each other to see who would mate with the females. Millions of years later, some animals, such as deer and hares, still behave like this before mating.

A large male **Vulcanodon** would gather a small group of females. Other large males then challenged him, probably roaring and tearing up the ground with their front legs. Circling around and around, one male would try to get close to the females.

When she was ready to lay her eggs, the female probably scraped a shallow nest in the ground. Then, squatting down, she would drop her eggs into it. Each egg was about the size of a very large grapefruit, and she may have laid six to eight at a time.

She may then have covered the eggs carefully with sand and left them to hatch in the sun.

The herd leader then charged at him, reaching out his long neck. When they were close enough, the two males may have reared up on their hind legs, lashing out at each other with their front legs. This fight may have gone on for several hours until the smaller, weaker male gave in, lumbering away, defeated.

The herd probably stayed close to the nest to guard it from predators. Soon after the babies broke out of the shells, they would be up and about on their legs and growing rapidly.

To mate with a female, the male probably stood on his hind legs, resting his front legs on her back and slightly to one side of her tail, the way elephants do.

19

Vulcanodon data

Vulcanodon was one of the giant plant-eaters that lived in Africa about 195 million years ago. Herds of these peaceful dinosaurs roamed the landscape in search of food, carefully guarding their young against predators.

Known for its huge, bulky body and rounded back, **Vulcanodon** walked slowly on all four stumpy legs. Under its skin there must have been powerful muscles and a big stomach to hold all the food it needed.

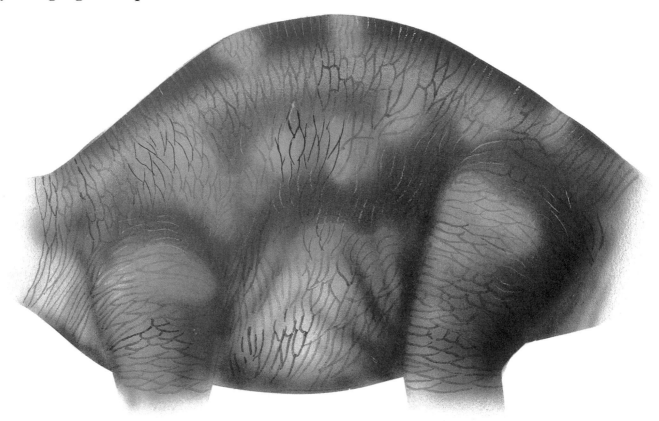

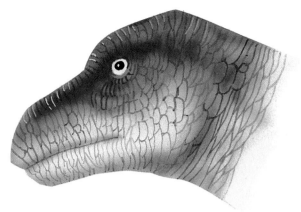

Mystery head

Although scientists found the skeleton of most of the body of **Vulcanodon**, the head was missing. But by looking at other members of the same family, scientists have decided that **Vulcanodon**'s head must have been quite small. Since there would not have been much room for a large brain, it was probably not very intelligent.

Chunky feet

Vulcanodon's feet were thick, each with four short toes. It also had one curved claw on the inside of each foot. It may have used this as a weapon when attacked. The males may also have used it when fighting during the mating season.

Long tail and neck

Vulcanodon's tail was long, thick, and heavy. It helped balance the weight and length of the long neck scientists believe **Vulcanodon** must have had.

Leathery skin

The skin of this dinosaur is likely to have been thick and leathery, like the skin of an

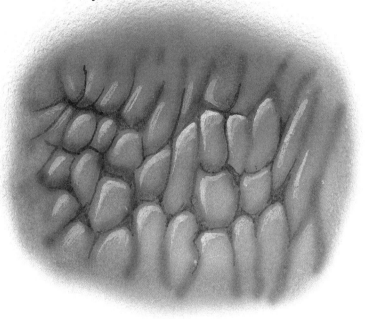

elephant, with lots of folds and creases. Such heavy skin was very useful for protecting **Vulcanodon** from thorny vegetation and trees, and also from biting insects.

More Jurassic plant-eaters

Vulcanodon (1), as we have seen, was one of the many large, plant-eating dinosaurs that lived in different parts of the world in Jurassic times. They probably all lived in herds that were always on the move in search of the huge amounts of food they needed to grow and survive. Let's now meet some of the other Jurassic plant-eaters.

Remains of Jurassic plant-eaters have been discovered around the world. One of the oldest Chinese dinosaurs from Early Jurassic times was **Lufengosaurus** (LOO-<u>FENG</u>-OH-<u>SAW</u>-RUS) (**2**). It was as long as a city bus and had a small head, along with a long neck and tail.

A dinosaur not yet officially named but for the moment known as **Supersaurus** (<u>SOO</u>-PER-<u>SAW</u>-RUS) (**3**) may have been one of the largest plant-eaters of all. Only a few bones have been found in Colorado, but one — a shoulder blade — is as tall as a man.

Barapasaurus (BA-<u>RA</u>-PA-<u>SAW</u>-RUS) (**4**) has a name meaning "big leg." This name was given to it by a truck driver who helped transport some of its bones. Its skeleton was first discovered in central India, but the bones were spread across many fields. It is one of the oldest dinosaurs of the **Sauropod** family found so far. But, as this picture shows, like **Vulcanodon**, it was small when compared to **Supersaurus**!

Massospondylus (<u>MASS</u>-OH-<u>SPOND</u>-IH-LUS) (**5**) was even smaller in comparison — about 13 feet (4 m) long from what is now South Africa. Like most of the Jurassic plant-eaters, it had a long neck and tail, and strong back legs. And like **Vulcanodon**, it also had a large, curved claw on each foot.

4

5

GLOSSARY

carnivores — meat-eating animals.

extinction — the dying out of all members of a plant or animal species.

fossils — traces or remains of plants and animals found in rock.

herbivores — plant-eating animals.

herd — a group of animals that travels together.

mate (v) — to join together (animals) to produce young.

offspring — the babies, or young, of an animal or plant.

paleontologists — scientists who study the remains of plants and animals that lived millions of years ago.

predators — animals that kill other animals for food.

quadrupeds — animals with four feet.

remains — a skeleton, bones, or dead body.

INDEX